28 TIPS FOR TEENAGERS

LIFE SKILLS THAT FAST TRACK SUCCESS

CRAIG GODDARD

First published in 2017 by Grammar Factory Pty Ltd.

© Craig Goddard, 2017

The moral rights of the author have been asserted

All rights reserved. Except as permitted under the Australian Copyright Act 1968 (for example, a fair dealing for the purposes of study, research, criticism or review), no part of this book may be reproduced, stored in a retrieval system, communicated or transmitted in any form or by any means without prior written permission.

All inquiries should be made to the author.

National Library of Australia Cataloguing-in-Publication entry:

> Creator: Goddard, Craig, author.
> Title: 28 things I wish I knew when I was a teenager / Craig Goddard.
> ISBN: 9780995445352 (paperback)
> Subjects: Teenagers--Life skills guides.
>   Youth--Conduct of life.
>   Adolescent psychology.

Printed in Australia by Minuteman Press Prahran

Cover and character design by Ally Pedersen

Book production and editorial services by Grammar Factory

Disclaimer

The material in this publication is of the nature of general comment only, and does not represent professional advice. It is not intended to provide specific guidance for particular circumstances and it should not be relied on as the basis for any decision to take action or not take action on any matter which it covers. Readers should obtain professional advice where appropriate, before making any such decision. To the maximum extent permitted by law, the author and publisher disclaim all responsibility and liability to any person, arising directly or indirectly from any person taking or not taking action based on the information in this publication.

CONTENTS

Introduction ... 5

SCHOOL AND WORK

1 Cool kids don't matter ... 11
2 Teachers know a lot, but not everything ... 15
3 Get a part-time job ... 21
4 Say lots without opening your mouth ... 27
5 What comes after school? ... 33
6 Your first job is not a life sentence ... 39
7 University = success, true or false? ... 43
8 Seek challenges and promotion ... 49
9 Chase a happy workplace – not just money ... 55

LIFE

10 Be on time ... 63
11 How should I talk to this person? ... 67
12 Please do it now ... 73
13 'I don't mind.' ... 77
14 Talking versus texting ... 83
15 Did we sort that out? ... 89

16	Plan before you move out of home	93
17	Find mentors and advisors	97
18	Ask that question	101
19	Be politely determined	105
20	Can they help me succeed?	111
21	Go straight there – not sideways	115

ADVANCED

22	Keep your moods to yourself	121
23	Listen before you speak	127
24	Treat everybody as important	131
25	Cuddle angry people into happiness	135
26	Treat others like yourself	139
27	Always praise people	145
28	Say thank you often	149

Conclusion	153
About the author	155
Acknowledgements	157

INTRODUCTION

I love seeing young adults achieve their full potential.

Whatever that potential is, it shouldn't be measured against anyone else. Every individual has their own unique potential, and the fulfilment of that potential depends on how each person approaches the world.

If I had known when I was younger what I'm about to share with you now, my journey would have been much easier.

For nearly two decades I have owned and managed a large number of Subway sandwich stores, which employ hundreds of teenagers. People like you have dominated a large part of my life. I genuinely enjoy the company of teenagers and they keep me on my toes as I continue to learn from them.

My journey in life, which includes my career, has been one of evolution rather than a well thought-out or conventional pathway. But I have always followed some simple rules and philosophies in the hope that my different approach would eventually see me achieve whatever plan I had at that time. My main focus has always been to identify the outcome I was seeking, work out how I should best conduct myself, and then work with the people involved to get the result I desired. For the most part, I have got the results I wanted.

I would say I have been fortunate, as a non-traditional route is not always the easiest one to follow. But it does offer many life experiences and lessons that aren't taught in school.

In this book I share some of the strategies I have had success with personally, both while I was at school and when I was starting in business, together with my observations of the many young people I have employed and been able to support. In this book you will find twenty-eight tips, ideas, lessons – whatever you like to call them – that I have learnt on my unconventional journey through life. I have divided them into three categories:

- School and work
- Life
- Advanced

You can read the book from start to finish if you like, or you can look for a section that you think will help your situation, or you can dip in and out at random. It really doesn't matter, and whether you read all the tips or just one or two, I'm confident that you will find a helpful suggestion.

I continue to work with, listen to, and seek to support the aspirations of teenagers. It is my sincere hope that you find some useful advice in this book.

Enjoy,
Craig.

SCHOOL AND WORK

What you will do when you finish school is likely to be dominating your thoughts. How to survive in school, make a plan for your career and, once you get there, make the most of your opportunities are all issues that you might need support with.

1

Cool kids don't matter

[READ THIS IF YOU'RE A BIT OF AN OUTSIDER OR IF YOU GET TEASED OR BULLIED.]

When I was at school there was never any chance of me being in the 'cool group'. I was shy, a bit chubby, had bright red hair and lots of freckles, and wore big black-rimmed glasses. I looked like Ron Weasley out of the Harry Potter movies.

At one stage I moved schools mid-year. My old school jumper was burgundy and the new school's was green. But my mother decided that it wasn't worth buying a new jumper until I had grown out of my old one, so I had to wear the wrong uniform for the rest of the school year. Just when I wanted to belong and blend in, I had to walk around the school looking like nobody else in a jumper that clashed with my hair colour. It was not a good start and, as you would expect, I got teased.

I'm sure those of you who are not part of the cool group and are bullied or just labelled as 'different' could share similar stories. The good news is that I now know that being cool is irrelevant. Although it's difficult to handle not being invited to parties or being singled out in some other way, it's not forever.

I was lucky because I worked this out when I was at high school and tried to spend time with people who had similar interests to mine and who accepted me for who I was.

I was so much happier and it removed a lot of unnecessary stress. It's funny to think back now, but we were our own cool group: four of us in a deserted corner of the schoolyard, happy with our own stuff, discussing Star Trek, environmental sustainability, or whether there's life on other planets. There were still times when I was bullied, but I had friends that I could turn to and talk about the bad times with and it seemed to make things easier.

Any relevance the cool group has ends once you leave school, and they soon find out that bullying is totally unacceptable in the adult world. In fact, one of the boys I really wanted to accept me became part of the wrong crowd after school and has spent time in prison. Others I know have simply bounced from job to job with no real ambition to succeed at anything other than hanging on to being cool.

But the three friends I spent endless hours with in that deserted corner of the playground are all successful. One is a pilot with Qantas, the second works in the US as a senior programmer with IBM, and the third is the chief accountant for a large ethical investment company!

But while you're waiting impatiently for the future to arrive, we can't ignore what may be going on for you right now. It can be hard to put up with being teased and left out of things, but you can do things to make it easier. Remove any unpleasant people from your focus and look at the things you can control: be with people who like you the way you are, study hard, and enjoy planning for life after high school.

> **The so-called cool group's relevance expires when they leave school. These people have had their moment of glory and soon it will be your turn.**

Teachers know a lot, but not everything

[READ THIS IF YOU'RE SCARED OF YOUR TEACHERS.
OR IF YOU LIKE YOUR TEACHERS.
OR IF YOU THINK THEY'RE A BIT WEIRD.]

Much of our early time on this planet is spent in the company of teachers who, along with our parents or guardians, form the backbone of how we learn.

I'm a little embarrassed to say that much of what I learnt at school has faded from my middle-aged memory banks, but I do remember many of my teachers, both the good and the bad. Now, as a parent, I see how hard they work and the massive influence they can have. Teachers, like their students, are all individuals – there are some you will connect with and learn a great deal from, and others not so much. As a result, if you like a subject, or if the teacher makes it interesting, it's much more likely you will absorb what's being said.

In Year 5 I had a young teacher who was full of enthusiasm and encouragement, and really took an interest in each of us. This certainly gave me confidence and I really wanted to listen and learn. But the following year was a complete contrast. My teacher was approaching retirement and was constantly grumpy. He was an ex-army sergeant and had a one-size-fits-all style of teaching. He sat boys and girls on different sides of the classroom and controlled the class with a loud voice and threats of the cane. I remember little from that year other than being scared.

Then on to secondary school and instead of having one teacher, there were different teachers for every subject. They had a variety of personalities and outside interests, many of which found their way into the classroom. As their views tended to be delivered with authority and in the classroom setting, those views could be adopted by their students too – for better or worse. Some teachers can be very passionate about their subjects and even jokingly promote their topic at the expense of another. They might say things like, 'History is interesting, but maths is vital.'

The danger of this is that it might encourage you in a direction that you don't find interesting or that just isn't important for you. Of course, I'm not saying you shouldn't try to do your best in subjects you don't like. What I mean here is that you shouldn't choose a direction you feel is wrong for you, or panic if a supposedly 'vital' subject is not one of your strengths. Let me explain:

One of my children had one such maths teacher. At a parent-teacher meeting, I was confronted by a grim-faced man with his arms crossed in front of a ridiculously neat suit. I noticed on a page of names that my son's was the only one highlighted. He went on to explain that he was extremely concerned about my son and his lack of ability in maths. 'How is he going to get on in the world?' he asked. I replied that my wife and I both found maths confusing and difficult. Although we would encourage our son to do his best, we didn't see it as a major problem and we both had successful careers despite our struggles with maths.

That teacher's opinion was just that – an opinion, not a fact.

I know many very successful people who really struggled with things at school; I like to call them 'non-traditional academics'. They're good at many things, just not what they teach you at school. Some of you may have heard of Lindsay Fox, a successful businessman who left school before completing Year 10 and started driving a truck. He now runs Linfox, which he built up with lots of determination, hard work and entrepreneurial skill to become the largest privately owned trucking company in Australia. As early as you can, start looking for people who can add to what you learn at school – people who you find interesting and stimulating.

Teachers are important while you're serving your 'apprenticeship' for the adult world. Listen carefully, try your hardest and absorb all you can, but don't worry if a subject is not for you. Instead, spend time developing your strengths and working out how you may be able to build on these in search of a career.

> **Learn all you can, and value the advice passed on by your teachers but, as with any advice, always question whether it's right for you, seek other opinions and follow your strengths.**

Get a part-time job

READ THIS WHETHER YOU WANT A JOB OR NOT.
GO ON, IT'S ONLY A COUPLE OF PAGES.

Some want to, others need to, and plenty should.

You can invent plenty of reasons why you shouldn't get a part-time job:

- 'I've got too much homework.'
- 'I can't be bothered.'
- 'There are no jobs around.'
- 'The pay is hopeless.'
- 'I have too much sport.'
- 'I have no way of getting there.'
- 'Blah blah blah…'

Some parents would prefer their teenagers didn't work, and they've got a fresh list of reasons:

- 'It might affect your school work.'
- 'There's no time after music and sport.'
- 'I'm not a taxi service.'
- 'Do a few jobs around the house and I'll give you pocket money.'
- 'Blah blah blah…'

Do not listen to your parents (on this topic)!

Having worked with hundreds of teenagers, I am yet to see a situation where even the busiest student cannot successfully fit a part-time job into their schedule. In my view, the benefits far outweigh any compromise that has to be made. It's like an apprenticeship for adult life that highlights the differences between school and the workplace and helps prepare you for them.

Decision made! Let's get started – with three simple steps:

- Get some help with preparing a resume.
- Get it out there *in person*.
- Hand out as many as you can.

It's also a good idea to practise how you're going to present yourself to potential employers, and you should find later chapters in the book helpful with this. It may take many resumes and many interviews, but be determined.

Got a job? What now?

Once you have a job, you might find that people have new expectations of you, and you may need to make some changes.

The first thing you should do is start some sort of a diary so that you can see all your commitments and can plan ahead. No wasted time: be organised.

If you aren't able to drive yourself, getting to work may be your first attempt at public transport and having to be strictly on time. There is nothing worse than arriving to grumpy workmates who have had to stay back to cover for you while your boss angrily taps his watch.

A part-time job is also a trial run for what it will be like when you're in the permanent workforce. You must learn to get on with people from different backgrounds, work as part of a team, and sometimes make sacrifices for the sake of others. You may encounter a sort of friendship different from what you knew at school. There may be difficult times as well, but most workplaces have their own forms of support and encouragement.

In our Subway stores we have a sort of a mantra that says we treat each other with respect, and I highlight this at every new-staff orientation. We applaud people's strengths and support any struggles they might have. Being cool is irrelevant; you are simply part of a team. Maybe this helps explain why our staff tend to stay at Subway – many have formed friendship groups and don't see coming to work as something to dread.

The best part of having a job is that you get paid, and with pay comes your first taste of independence. When you have money of your own, you can choose to save it or spend it. I suspect you might surprise yourself with how carefully you spend and appreciate your money when you earn it yourself, rather than when it's handed to you.

Getting a part-time job can also launch a whole career. It certainly helped set up a career for this employee:

Alan came to work with me as a no-frills fifteen-year-old who spoke his mind with no fuss (another staff member put it perfectly by saying he doesn't put up with any crap). Despite not being a textbook potential employee, he appeared honest and enthusiastic during his interview so we gave him an opportunity to work at Subway.

As time went on we focused on improving his bluntness with customers, getting him to speak more clearly, helping him manage his fluctuating moods and ensuring he kept his uniform presentable. To his credit he responded to our concerns and improved in all areas.

I continued to give him challenges and he ultimately progressed to being a store manager. We still focused on small improvements, giving praise and acknowledgement when these were achieved.

He was excellent in dealing with challenging staff and we often sent difficult staff to the store that Alan managed to get them back on track, which he usually did. I remember acknowledging one such success, and in passing suggested he would be a natural as a social worker.

Despite some initial doubt, Alan enrolled in an appropriate course and we were able to structure his work hours around his study. He completed the course and we put a resume together, did mock interviews, and suggested how he might approach the positions he was applying for. He was ultimately successful and now works as a youth social worker.

Alan's decision to get a part-time job ended up being life changing. He was able to work on areas of his personality that needed finetuning, develop his people management skills and find a career that fitted him perfectly.

> **From small beginnings, happy, satisfying careers can grow.**

Say lots without opening your mouth

READ THIS IF YOU'RE SHY AND THINK NOBODY NOTICES YOU.

You can say a lot without opening your mouth. It doesn't matter whether it's someone you see often or someone you're meeting for the first time; you can create a presence, tone and mood for yourself without saying a word. Whether you're walking towards friends, facing an opponent on the sporting field or approaching a panel for a job interview, you can convey a lot about yourself and how you're feeling before you even speak.

This is particularly important for a job interview, so I want to give you some tips on what you can do to create the best possible silent first impression.

Dress to impress

If you turn up to a job interview in trendy street clothes, the majority of the time you will already have a cross through your name.

A good rule is to wear clothes that are similar to the ones you would wear if you got the job. If it's a fast food restaurant that has a uniform, wear clean, dark pants or a skirt, a neat shirt (keep the bra straps out of sight) and smart shoes. It is not necessary to wear a suit or to dress up; save this for when you go for a position where that's the normal dress code.

Remember that this is probably the most powerful tool you have. I recently saw my fifteen-year-old son in a suit for the first time and it was a real eye opener ... he was suddenly all grown up.

Walk the walk

This is super important. If I'm doing job interviews and someone walks in slouching and with no purpose in their step, my first thought is 'unmotivated'. In contrast, if you stand tall and walk briskly and purposefully towards me, with your hand out ready for a firm handshake (both male and female), you will impress.

When you sit down, do it with care. Sit up straight with your hands on the table in front of you – this shows you're giving the business in hand your full attention. If you're standing, make sure your feet and body are pointing at the person interviewing you and make gentle eye contact. This illustrates that you're listening fully.

Look like you mean it

You can set so many different and subtle moods with the expression on your face. Again, think about who you're approaching and what the right expression is for the moment. I've noticed that when my children walk into a room, they're often expressionless until they know the mood. Do not approach an interview in such a manner. Instead, have your eyes wide open when you enter the room and look at the person who will interview you with enthusiasm. Offer a warm smile when you're introduced. During your interview maintain a natural, interested expression. But don't be over the top: fake enthusiasm is a negative.

Be fragrant

This is a slightly delicate topic, but personal hygiene is very important. I'm not suggesting you over-do the perfume or after-shave, but be freshly showered and well groomed, without too much make-up or jewellery. This shows you're trying your best.

In complete contrast to all of these points was this interview I conducted just recently:

> *This candidate arrived in skater clothes. Everything was too big and baggy and he struggled as he walked in my direction. He appeared uninterested and looked everywhere except at me. However, I put that to one side and we began the interview. While we were talking,*

I heard several beeps: a text message had arrived for him. That's okay – everyone forgets to turn their phone off sometimes. But to my complete surprise, for the next couple of minutes he repeatedly glanced down between his legs to try to 'secretly' read the text. Needless to say he didn't get the job.

This one certainly said plenty without opening his mouth.

> **Take the time and effort to not only prepare for what you will say, but also how you will approach others physically. It's an important part of the impression you give.**

5

What comes after school?

READ THIS IF YOU DON'T KNOW WHAT YOU WANT TO DO WHEN YOU LEAVE SCHOOL. OR IF YOU'VE SIGNED UP FOR THE FIRST COURSE YOU THOUGHT OF DOING. OR WERE ACCEPTED INTO THE COURSE THAT EVERYBODY ELSE THINKS YOU SHOULD DO.

When I was young, I got used to being asked, 'What would you like to do when you leave school?' I suspect it's as annoying for you as it was for me, especially if you don't have an answer. Saying, 'I don't know,' or, 'I haven't given it any thought yet,' can buy you some time, but won't make the question go away altogether. And eventually you will have to answer the question for yourself.

A way to get started, if you have no idea, is to look at the people around you and the jobs they do. See if you can picture yourself in that role and ask lots of questions. If it's interesting, speak to people who work in that field and ask questions about job satisfaction, opportunities to advance, and how they got to where they are. Your mission is not to find a course to study, but rather to identify a job or career that feels right for you. Working out what study is required comes later.

The next and most important task: check out job prospects now and in the future. If there are few opportunities, maybe you need to rethink. On the other hand, if you're interested in the job and it has reasonable prospects, now is when you check whether study is required. Do not choose a course and hope there is a job at the end.

By taking this approach, you are more likely to avoid the wasted time and expense of studying a course because 'I was good at those subjects' or 'I got the marks' or 'I was sort of interested in it' with no idea of a job, its prospects, where it will lead you or whether you will find it satisfying.

This can happen all too easily. Perhaps you're top of the class in sciences and are seen as doctor material. On the other hand, you're also very good with your hands and have a long-held ambition to be a cabinetmaker. Others will be likely to pressure you to follow a certain pathway, but you might decide that the best option is the one you will enjoy and that gives you a lifestyle that's right for you. Doing your research and working out a plan will help you be clear about what you want and resist this type of pressure. Start with the career counsellor at school, and then there's my lifelong friend Mr Google – there aren't many questions he can't find answers to.

But what if, despite all your research, you still have no idea, no career and no direction? Or maybe you've just finished Year 12 and deferred from a course that doesn't interest you, but everybody else thinks it's the most obvious and best option. Perhaps you don't think university is right for you at this stage. What do you do? It's important to remember that a career can come out of left field, so just keep thinking, planning and observing. Let me explain.

> Izzy had a job with a major retailer that she really enjoyed. She even privately thought that she was more competent than some of the senior employees and could see opportunities for herself. The store offered Izzy a full-time job with extra responsibility for her deferment year that she eagerly accepted. This year could have just come and gone, with Izzy heading off to a uni course at the end of it that she was not really interested in. But instead she thought outside the box and decided to explore where this job might take her. On her first day, Izzy made an appointment to speak to the senior person in recruitment and said that although she had a uni place waiting for her at the end of the year, it was not really where she wanted to be. She said that she enjoyed working with the retailer, was ambitious and felt that she had plenty to offer. Long story short, she did get a permanent position and some years later is now in senior management with that company.

You will never know unless you ask. You might think it's all too hard, but give it a go; opportunity is there for those who ask.

That's one story, and there are many other unconventional career paths. For example, sometimes your hobbies or interests can lead to a career.

> *Jane loved animals – especially dogs. She volunteered in an animal shelter and one of her jobs was to take the dogs for their daily walk. Friends of Jane's family heard about this and, feeling guilty about not taking their dogs for regular walks, asked her if she would be prepared to do this for a fee. At first she said she was happy to do it for free; however, on their insistence a fee was agreed on. Word got around and before Jane knew it, she had too many dogs to walk and even had to employ a helper. Jane noticed that many of her clients were young couples who worked long hours and lived in inner-city apartments. They were concerned about the lack of attention that their dogs were getting while they were at work all day. Recognising a need, Jane developed a business plan for a doggie kinder. Owners could drop off their pets on the way to work, and the dogs were washed, fed, groomed and walked. After work, guilt-free parents picked up their happy dogs, and took them home with nothing left to do but cuddle and play with them. The business thrived, now has several locations and is still growing.*

It may be that your obvious academic strengths lead you to a career. If not, explore opportunities that might come from your hobbies, interests and passions. Don't just take the obvious or easiest route for the sake of it – thoroughly explore all options.

6

Your first job is not a life sentence

READ THIS IF YOU'VE READ THE PREVIOUS SECTION AND YOU'RE STILL HAVING TROUBLE FIGURING OUT WHAT YOU WANT TO DO AFTER SCHOOL.

I get it, you're still stuck. So let's try rephrasing the question to, 'What would I like to do 'for a time' when I finish school?'

The decision you make today does not have to be for a lifetime, and if you are unable to plan for the next twenty years, try ten, or even five. But whatever you do, don't float around with no plan at all. In the past people could be in the one job forever, but today most people change jobs many times.

> *I know someone who was a good student with many plans who was constantly being asked about life after school. His mother and teachers were very keen for him to use his good marks and go to university. But he wasn't interested in further study at this stage. His father was a self-employed tradesman and he liked the idea of having his own business one day, and as he already knew about the job, he decided to commit to a three-year apprenticeship.*
>
> *As an apprentice, he worked hard and sought extra opportunities and training. As a result, he won 'Apprentice of the Year' through all three years of his training and won an international scholarship to go to the UK for further education. While overseas, he learnt all he could and looked for skills and opportunities to bring home. Back in Australia, he saw an opening in retail products*

allied with his trade, and opened a small store. This grew to two and then three stores and the business expanded to include importing products for the stores. Constantly looking for new challenges, he also partnered with others in a plant nursery and a liquor store.

Then came the loss of a close family member and with it, a new plan. He sold all his businesses and returned to full-time study, completed a course in health and began working in that field. This grew to having his own health-food store. Always looking to advance, he then joined a new food franchise, opened one store, then a second, third, fourth ... and continued to grow to a total of fourteen stores, with more than 200 staff!

Oh, and if you haven't guessed by now, that person was me.

> **If you're stuck on what to do, research what seems like a good plan for your foreseeable future, one you can see yourself doing at least for a while, then work hard and seek opportunities. If circumstances change, be prepared to start that process again, and if it requires more education, go for it and make that transition while committing in the same way. Life is a journey and your career choice does not need to be forever.**

7

University = success true or false?

READ THIS IF YOU THINK UNIVERSITY IS A MAGIC WAND.

When I was at high school, going to university was not as common as it is today and somehow seemed harder to achieve. Maybe it was because there were fewer degrees on offer, or perhaps there was a different emphasis on education. One thing's for sure – getting a job and building a career is a changing game. But is it really necessary to have a uni degree?

In the past there were many jobs that required no further study; you got a job and were trained in what you needed to know. If you were a strong communicator with good people skills, you might have got a job in a department store, worked in different departments and ended up in management. Similarly, you may have started in the bank as a teller and progressed to manager. These career paths are all still available today and, although you may need to add some tertiary education along the way, 'growing' into your ultimate role is a real pathway and certainly worth considering.

There were once also more careers that did require training, but not at university; TAFE courses and apprenticeships were more common. For example, learning to become a nurse was more like an apprenticeship – you started your nursing straight after high school, all training was done in the hospital and you sat your exams there as well. Nowadays, it's a full-time university course.

In those days more of the courses were targeted and graduates were more likely to get a job in their area of study. Further education after high school was more about deciding on a career and studying the appropriate course, rather than studying something and working out what to do with it later.

That's something that's changed a lot. Now there's a range of modern degree courses, such as exercise physiology or computer-game writing, that are more like study areas than job-specific courses. Courses like sports journalism often have far more graduates than jobs available, and I frequently receive resumes from frustrated graduates from these and other similar courses.

One concern today is that there are increasing numbers of students who go to university with no particular job in mind or, if they do have one in mind, haven't researched if positions are likely to be available when they graduate. Instead, they enrol in their course because, 'It's what I got the marks to get into,' 'It doesn't look too hard,' or 'I have no idea what I want to do so I thought I'd do this.'

Too often this ends in no job, study debt or even multiple degree dropouts.

But let's return to the question: Does University = Success? For me, the answer is: Not automatically.

You should be careful about doing a degree just to get a qualification with no real position as a target. But if the course you're looking at is in an area you genuinely enjoy and has reasonable job prospects, and you have spoken to people in that job, then go for it. While you are studying, chase work experience or a relevant part-time job – anything that can put you ahead of others with the same degree. And remember that there are many pathways to success, such as TAFE, apprenticeships, or working your way up while employed.

My point is this: identify a career you are interested in, do your research, speak to people working in that area and confirm that there are jobs available. If you need a university qualification, go for it: study hard, network, seek industry mentors and work experience. But if you don't think university is right for you, remember that there are alternatives.

Here's a ripper 'non-university' success story:

Angus had always struggled with traditional subjects but excelled in the creative arts and drama, and was a fantastic communicator. However, as he was at a school where the majority of students attended university, there was always that expectation that he would also go to uni. While Angus was in Year 9 at high school his family sold their home. The process fascinated him; the need to build relationships, communicate well and maintain a negotiating edge excited him and he felt he could do well in these areas. At the end of the sale process he announced, 'I could do that job.' When Angus completed Year 12 he still liked the idea of being a real estate agent, so he spoke to people in the industry to better understand what was involved. This only confirmed his resolve, but under the pressure and expectation of his school and parents, Angus reluctantly enrolled in a marketing degree. 'This will be useful if you eventually do real estate,' they said. Six months into his course, Angus decided university wasn't for him and applied for jobs in the real estate industry. Within a month he had three job offers. Fast-forward seven years and Angus is now one of the most successful young agents in his town and a director of the company.

> Not having a degree does not mean you will automatically be less successful than someone who does. It's much more about making smart career choices, having a good attitude and constantly looking for opportunities.

Seek challenges and promotion

READ THIS IF YOU WANT TO GET AHEAD. OR NOT.

Whether you work on the checkouts at the supermarket, on the counter in a fast food chain or on the bottom rung of a corporate ladder, the opportunity for promotion is something you can influence. Set your goals, and start getting the attention of the people in your workplace who can help you achieve these.

But first, a word of warning. It's important that your efforts to get ahead are seen as genuine, not simply 'sucking up'. This could see you slide back down the ladder, as well as make you unpopular with other staff.

Right, warning done. Now for the plan.

The plan

- Get clear about what you want to achieve. For example, do you hope to move from the checkout register to the customer-care counter? Do you know how to close a store but want to learn how to open?

- Think about what that new role involves. Do some self-assessment and see things through the eyes of your boss: are you ready to progress?

- Arrange a formal time to have a meeting so your boss is focused on what you have to say; it's unlikely you will get a good hearing if you try discussing things when it's busy.

- During the meeting, tell the boss what you identified in the first point above – don't make them guess. Tell them it's something you would really like to aim for. Then confirm what skills are required to progress and whether there are any areas you need to improve.

- Ask the boss whether they would mind spending some extra time with you on training or whether you could work in a different area to gain more experience.

You may get some initial encouragement, but your glorious career advancement may not be high on the boss's priority list. But even if the boss seems less than enthusiastic after your first discussion, at least you've created the impression of someone who is keen and willing to learn. You will be in a great position to try again another time.

Your career advancement now becomes a mission of polite, quiet persistence. Look for reasons to give your boss little reminders about your ambitions and let him or her know when you've ticked off achievements from the list of suggested improvements. If you're really keen, you might offer to stay back after work or come in early to watch and learn a new skill or procedure. It's unlikely you would be asked to, but it does show how committed you are. And if you're determined to progress in your job, but find there is little response despite trying all of the tactics discussed above, then maybe it's time to look elsewhere.

Here's the story of someone who followed this plan:

> We employed a rather quiet sixteen-year-old to work in one of our Subway stores. As we don't have 'back of house' at Subway, you're out serving customers from day one. This comes naturally for some, and they move from 'Trainee' to 'Sandwich Artist' quickly and get increased hours. But this new trainee was shy and unsure of herself, and customers struggled to hear her. Nonetheless, she was always on time and polite, and I could see she was listening to my suggestions. As she continued to improve she sought confirmation that she was on the right track.
>
> She was saving for a bike and keen to work extra hours, and I explained that to do this she would need to learn how to work the evening shifts. She asked if she could come in as an extra during a close to learn the procedure. She was there the next night and not long after filling that role, she took the same approach to learning store openings. She

finished Year 12 and deferred from university. Knowing we were about to open another store, she asked what she needed to do to become a store manager. Although she was younger than any manager we had employed before, her enthusiasm, willingness to learn and desire to progress meant she had earned the opportunity, so she was put on a learning fast-track with one of our senior managers. She did become that new store manager, and later an area manager with five stores. She never did take up that option for university, and ten years later she is still with us and runs the whole business for weeks on end while I'm away.

> **You too can achieve your goals but you must be determined. Once you achieve one, go after the next.**

Chase a happy workplace – not just money.

MONEY IS KING RIGHT? IF YOU THINK THAT'S TRUE, READ ON.

Let's say you've just turned fifteen, put together a resume, and begun to hand it round the fast food restaurants in your area. You hope someone will give you a chance so you can save to buy that motorbike, have money for a holiday, or just have some money of your own.

Now is not the time to be fussy; just go for it and take any job opportunity you're offered. Work hard, be enthusiastic and learn all you can.

On your journey through high school, and maybe later at university, you're likely to have several jobs and need them more and more. You might move out of home and have rent, food and transport to pay for, with maybe a bit left over to do what you like with. Your main focus is probably still to earn as much money as you can for as little work as possible. But this may not always be the case.

Perhaps you've just started a job at a 24-hour restaurant. You begin with a few hours a week and, because you're enthusiastic and always available, your hours increase. You're offered work on the overnight shift, which you're happy with because that pays the highest wages. Fast-forward twelve months and you're getting maximum hours on the highest hourly rate. It sounds great, but there's a problem. Your boss is rude, demanding, and unappreciative. The customers who come in at night-time are often drunk and abusive, and you don't get on that well with the night staff. What's more, you've now worked in every area of the restaurant and on every possible shift. There's nothing more to learn.

What you're really after is a job in a quality cafe where you can learn how to make coffee and serve customers who appreciate the effort you put into service. The problem is that what you currently earn is as good as it gets, so you reluctantly think you had better just carry on.

Maybe you'll have to, at least for a while, but there's no harm in looking for an alternative.

What you need to do is stick with your current job, but redo your resume with your new experience and highlight the areas that you think might help land your target job. Dress in clothing appropriate for the job and visit all the local cafes. Ask to speak to the manager so you can hand over your resume in person. Briefly say that you're keen for an opportunity, have hospitality experience and are willing to come in for a trial any time. If you have no luck, wait about a month, then visit all the cafes again and hand in another resume.

Then success: a week later you get a call, an interview, and you get the job. The owner seems friendly, is happy to teach you coffee making, and the cafe is in a nice end of town. Sounds perfect? The problem is that the pay is twenty per cent less than you're getting in your current, crappy job. So what do you do?

I'll tell you, along with a true story.

> *Paige needed the higher wage but she was really unhappy in her existing work, so she took the cafe job and immediately started looking for ways to cut her spending. She started her new job full of energy and was soon being offered plenty of hours. Because she gave great customer service, she was also getting extra money from generous tips. With maximum hours, spending cuts and tips, the shortfall in wages was covered. Just as importantly, it was altogether a better and happier place to work. The other staff were great and Paige was able to learn coffee making, how to open and close the cafe, and*

some management skills. Paige went on to own and run her own very successful cafe and restaurant.

> **If you're unhappy at work, don't stay for the sake of it; have a go at finding an alternative. It may not be possible, but job satisfaction, new experience and skills in an area that interest you can be worth more than just the money.**

LIFE

Okay, so we have made a good start on some school strategies and getting a plan for later. Now let's have a look at some life skills, many of which you can choose to use at school, but most of which are non-negotiable in the adult world.

Be on time

READ THIS IF YOU'RE NOT, USUALLY.

Be on time. Three very simple words, but a failure to observe them can have complicated and unfortunate results.

Before starting school, time is pretty much irrelevant. There was night and day and the main reason you did anything was because you were told you had to – it didn't matter what the time was.

Then it was off to primary school where the school bell ruled your day. You probably had no idea what time it was – you just knew you had to go straight to class when it rang. Usually, the consequences for being late were relatively small.

Next, secondary school begins and things get a little more complicated. The bell is still there, but classes are now in several different rooms. The day may not divide into three neat sections, like in primary school, and classes may be different lengths without a strict pattern. Being late could see you greeted by an angry teacher who has had to delay the start of class until you arrived, or worse, they might start, then stop when you arrive so the class can give you a cheer on arrival. At worst, you could get detention or feel embarrassed. But still no real damage done.

If you begin university, the relevance of time and knowing where you should be really starts to get serious. There's no bell to remind you, lectures are all over the place and sometimes at different campuses. You might have an online tutorial this week and one on campus the next. There is no-one reminding you where you should be and when; it's completely up to you whether you arrive or not. The responsibility for being late, missing a lecture, a compulsory tutorial or even an exam is yours, and not being on time has real consequences.

When you start looking for work, being on time is absolutely crucial. Being late can even cost you a job. Maybe you're looking for part-time work and arrive five minutes late for your interview. The person who was scheduled after you arrived early and has been taken in first. Based on my experience, you may as well not bother attending this interview, as there is very little chance you will get the job. But if you arrive fifteen minutes early; you may be the one taken in first and get ahead in the race for that job. At the very least, it will give you time to gather your thoughts, relax, and think about what you want to say.

Being late can even cost you money. You might decide to take a gap year and travel, and let's say your first adventure is a flight to Sydney. You estimate how long it should take to get to the airport, but then sleep in because you're just not used to having to set an alarm. You don't wake up until your mate rings the doorbell, and after rushing to throw on some clothes and toss some more in a suitcase, you end up hitting peak hour traffic and don't get to the check-in until twenty-five minutes before departure – five minutes after the deadline. No matter how much you plead with the agent on the desk, they will not let you on the plane. As a result, instead of a $69 flight, you have to either purchase another two tickets for the next available flight at $325 each or miss the concert that night ... the tickets for which cost $295. There are definite consequences here.

> **Although it may not seem so important now, being aware of when you need to be on time (and not just in time) can make your life a lot smoother. Make never being late your priority – now.**

11

How should I talk to this person?

READ THIS IF YOU GET TONGUE-TIED WHEN YOU TALK TO PEOPLE, OR IF YOU TALK TOO MUCH.

To get the best outcome when speaking to people, you should avoid having a 'one-size-fits-all' approach to conversation. We are all unique, and should be spoken to as individuals.

But why is this important? You might be thinking, 'Isn't it up to others to take me as I am?' This might be acceptable for people who know you, but for those you have just met and are looking to impress, your normal approach may not always work. The success you have in job interviews and in sales or professional meetings, as well as day-to-day conversations, is often determined by your ability to speak to that person in a way that is appropriate.

This is not always easy, because you might feel intimidated if you're not as well educated as the person you're talking to or if you come from a different background. You might 'freeze' and not really know what to say. However, with some thought and practice, you can learn to comfortably start a conversation with almost anyone.

From a very young age, my mother insisted I adjust the way I spoke to all people so that I had a respectful tone. This is a good place to start, and this alone can make a big difference. When we meet people we usually form an initial opinion of them. So try to pause and think, based on that quick assessment, how you should speak to them to make them feel comfortable and get the best response.

The fact that we're all unique may have you wondering how you can possibly work out how to approach everyone. One strategy is to create smaller categories of people who have many similarities and use this as your starting point, fine tuning as you go. This method is used with new staff at Subway. Often it's their first job and first direct experience with people outside family and friends. It can be daunting and they may be intimidated, frightened or unsure. However, this approach helps them to feel more comfortable.

To keep it simple we have four groups – there are many more, but we will use these as a starting point. You can give some thought later to which other groups may be appropriate for you.

Older retired people

Young people often struggle with this group as they can be hard of hearing, get confused by too many choices, and are sometimes a bit grumpy. As one of our staff discovered, they do not necessarily respond well to, 'G'day mate.' The next time this staff member had an older customer, he used the approach that we taught him. First he caught the customer's eye, smiled and said clearly and slowly, 'Good afternoon sir, what bread would you like?' He could tell straight away that he was onto a winner. I happened to be in the store for both of those visits and the contrast in happiness for both the customer and the staff member was enormous.

Tradesmen

These are generally no-fuss people who want you to speak clearly and with plenty of volume. Don't ask more questions than necessary and listen carefully – they don't like having to say something twice. Be open to having a bit of a laugh with them, too.

School children

You may think this is an easy group to deal with because they're a similar age to you, and should have the same sense of humour. But my observations tell me this is not always the case, particularly when you're selling them something. For some reason their manner in the store is different from a social meeting. They can try to be 'smart' and show off in front of their friends. We suggest keeping it really simple and friendly without drawing attention to yourself.

Parents

Most of our staff find this the easiest group to talk to as they seem to have few hassles. There's a broad age range and the group can include anyone who seems old enough to be your parents, right through to young grandparents. They tend to know what they want and are not particularly moody or fussy. They often have children with them or are used to being around kids. They're happy just to get a smile from you and relaxed, but efficient service.

These are, of course, just a few stereotypical groups of people, but with a bit of thought you can come up with your own categories. Write them down and think about how people in those groups might like you to speak to them so that they feel comfortable. If a certain approach seems to work well, make a note of it. And if something backfires, don't try it again.

> **I continue to work on being the best I can at communicating with people in a way that makes sense for them. Make a start now; I'm confident you will enjoy the results.**

Please do it now

READ THIS IS YOU'RE SICK OF BEING NAGGED.

This statement is simple, but so important.

When young people are asked to do something straight away, you might hear responses like:

- 'There's plenty of time.'
- 'I'll do it later.'
- 'What's the hurry?'
- 'Chill out.'

In my opinion, this approach is a big mistake. It's much better to do it right now. Why?

- Well, why not? You know it has to be done eventually, and by doing it now you spend far less time stressing about it or inventing reasons to put it off. Once you get it done you can forget about it.

- The details are fresh in your mind. If you genuinely can't do to it immediately, write it down so you don't forget exactly what you need to do and treat it as a priority.

- Delaying it won't make it go away. Even if it's something you don't want to do at all, like cleaning out the guinea pig cage or telling someone that they haven't been invited to your party.

- It's annoying for everyone. Imagine the frustration for your parents or teachers when they have to keep asking you to do the same thing over and over again.

- It can actually mess up your whole life. Maybe not now, while you're still a teenager, but in the adult world the consequences of delaying things can really heat up and important opportunities can disappear if you don't break the habit of putting things off.

One of my favourite examples of how things go wrong when you put things off is what happens when you receive a gift card. How many of you have forgotten about them until after they expire, when they've become worthless? The simple solution is to use them straight away – problem solved.

In my late teens I was around a 'didn't do it now' situation that convinced me to do things right now. I was playing senior Australian Rules football. Part of the fun was the stuff you did with your teammates off the field. Some of the boys liked the horses and liked to have a bet (not me, I thought money was too hard to earn to give away) – in particular our full forward whose uncle owned a horse. One night at training he announced that his uncle thought his horse was a good chance that weekend and had big odds that were worth a small, fun bet. As he was going to the races and the odds were better with a bookmaker at the track, we all put in a few dollars for a group bet. Maybe you can guess how this ends. He got to the races knowing that he had a bet to place for his twenty mates, but because it was one of the last races, there was no stress about the bet – he could do it later. Of course he forgot. The horse got over the line and won. It certainly wasn't a good time for him the next night at training when we all came looking for our winnings.

> **As hard as it may seem at the time, just do it now, get it off your mind and get on with the next thing.**

13

'I don't mind.'

READ THIS IF YOU'RE SCARED OF YOUR OWN OPINIONS OR HATE MAKING A DECISION.

How many times have you heard someone being given a choice and saying something like:

- 'Whatever.'
- 'I don't care.'
- 'You choose.'
- 'I don't mind.'

This strikes me as strange: the person usually does mind, so why is the non-committal response so common?

Maybe they haven't heard the question properly and don't want to ask to have it repeated. Perhaps they know the answer they really want to give isn't the one the asker wants. Or worse: they don't know the answer that's wanted and are too frightened to choose one in case it's wrong. Confusing, isn't it? Instead of making a choice, they try to figure out what the asker wants – a silly and sometimes annoying game. When I was a teenager, I thought I was being tested whenever my parents asked me to choose. I thought they'd already made a decision but asked me about what I wanted just to see what I would say and, if what I wanted was different, to see if I could I justify the change.

But sometimes, the offer to choose is an expression of friendship or a type of gift; it's the person choosing to put aside what they would truly prefer. In not making a decision, you deny them the pleasure of giving. So when you say 'I don't care', even though it may not have been your intention, you may come across as rude or offensive. The answer 'I don't care' is the worst thing you can say, as it can often be interpreted to mean that you're not interested or that the matter in hand is not important enough for you to spend time thinking about it – an answer definitely best avoided!

It's a good idea to break this habit while you're still a teenager, and home is the perfect place to practise expressing your honest opinions. It's a training ground for you to think before you speak, to be clear about your choices, and to be in a position to calmly explain why you hold certain preferences and opinions.

When asked to make a choice, follow these steps:

- Think
- Decide
- Offer your answer
- If asked, explain why

Start doing that now before 'I don't mind' becomes your standard answer as you move into adulthood. I can say from personal experience that if you don't, it can be a hard habit to break.

> When I was twenty I travelled to the UK to meet some family friends. I was warmly welcomed – a contrast to the freezing UK winter, which was the opposite of the Australian summer I had just left. Straight from the airport we drove to their home for Sunday lunch – a solid three-hour affair, with beer, wine and fabulous food. I felt warm, cosy and welcomed while the rain poured down outside. To my surprise, after coffee and chocolates, came the question, 'Would you like to get some fresh air, look at some of the countryside and take the dog for a walk?' In my head I was thinking, 'You have got to be kidding. It's wet, freezing, I'm super jet-lagged and totally full of food and wine. I would much rather stay here and take a nap.'
>
> So what did I say?
>
> 'I don't mind.'
>
> Without any delay came the response, 'Right then, let's put on our coats and boots and go!'
>
> I returned freezing, wet and unhappy.

Why did I do that?

Maybe I thought it would be offensive if I said, 'No thanks,' or maybe I was too tired to explain. Or had it just become a habitual answer for anything that was a little hard?

I could have said, 'I would love to at some stage, but I'm really jet-lagged and can't keep my eyes open; would you mind if I have a sleep?' This answer would have been met with understanding and a nice warm bed. It ticks all the boxes by acknowledging the question and giving a caring response: all would have been fine.

When people are given options, those who think them through and make decisions are often seen as leaders. Consequently, their opinions and advice are valued. This person can be you.

> **When asked to make a choice ... make one.**

14

Talking versus texting

READ THIS IF YOU'RE ADDICTED TO YOUR PHONE.

As there's now so much technology we can use to communicate, it probably seems a bit out of step to suggest you talk to people instead of texting or typing. I'm not suggesting you suddenly change all that you do; Snapchat, Instagram, texting and email can make things quick and easy, but they shouldn't be the only way you communicate.

In the business world, to avoid disputes, almost everything is put in an email, and at work I am emailing people constantly. But on some occasions, I think people either don't want to, or can't be bothered, to pick up the phone even though a short conversation may have been so much easier.

Talking directly to someone can also prevent mis-understandings. Have you ever received a text where you understand the words but you're not sure if there's a hidden meaning or tone? Even with carefully chosen words (and emoji), texts often can't replace what you might pick up in the tone or manner of someone's voice on the phone. When you actually speak to someone, you also have a chance to recognise early in a conversation whether you misunderstood, allowing you to change direction before too much damage is done.

I have also noticed that some people will hide behind a text. It's so easy to send something that's not ideal and then immediately turn your phone off. Maybe people do this out of fear of the response they might get, or perhaps they're simply too lazy to explain things properly. Whatever the reason, I'm sure you'll agree that it's annoying. In so many situations, speaking directly to the person would result in both a quicker and better outcome.

The classic Subway example of people hiding behind a text message is staff calling in sick. Everyone knows our policy is to call me – my mobile is always on and as I have all the staff phone numbers and rosters I can get onto it ASAP. In the early days people would do things like leave a message on the store phone or text an off-duty manager, but messages would be missed and the store would end up a staff member short. So we made a policy: call me direct. Simple, right? But apparently not! I still get the hide-behind-the-text message saying 'haven't got enough credit to call' or the old reliable 'lost my voice and can't speak'.

So it's obvious that there are times when talking is better and is the best type of communication for the situation. For example, some of the communication in our Subway stores is via text. Emphasis on some. We only allow texting for the exchange of information that needs no further discussion, such as, 'What time does my shift start?' or, 'Which store am I working at?' In these circumstances, it's a quick and easy way to sort things out. On the other hand, if the situation requires more information, such as when people want to switch shifts, a phone call is necessary so everyone's clear on the detail and there's no confusion.

What I'm suggesting is that you think about the best way to communicate to be understood completely or to get the outcome you desire; don't automatically send an email or text.

So here's the challenge – and it will be massive for many. Before you send a text, email or other non-verbal message, I want you to stop and think: 'What is the reason I'm not speaking to this person face to face or on the phone?' Is it because:

- 'I can't be bothered to speak to them.'

    I get this, and sometimes I feel that way too, but if you just get on with making the call and deal with it straight away, it's actually less hassle than trying to write a text that says what you're thinking. The bonus is the other person doesn't get the impression that you can't be bothered calling them.

- 'I want to hide and don't want to have to explain or justify.'

  I understand that there are things that go on every day that are awkward, emotional or just hard to handle, and when there's something that's hard to say, sending a text is easy. The trouble is that this often makes things worse. Words and their meanings get confused easily in a text, and it's usually obvious that you're texting just to avoid a proper discussion about the issue.

- 'I'm in a rush and haven't got time to speak.'

  This is simply a cop-out. If you were to add up the time it takes to think about and write the text, then answer the return questions, you'd see that it's quicker to call. If you're too busy to call now, do it as soon as possible. If it's urgent, just stop what you're doing and call.

- I'm at an appointment or meeting and can't speak but can text.'

  Here, you're not doing anything properly: you can't use your phone properly because you're in a meeting, and because you're messing with your phone you're ignoring the meeting. Turn off your phone and when there's a break in the meeting call or, if appropriate, text.

If any of the points above, or something similar, are your 'excuses' for texting rather than speaking, reconsider.

> You will be surprised how much time you save, how quickly you can solve any issues and how many opportunities may present themselves when you make the effort to talk to people.

Did we sort that out?

JUST READ THIS.

As a parent, this is a question I have heard on many occasions. The word 'we' is used to lessen the impact of forgetting something by sharing the responsibility with someone else, even though it has nothing to do with them. Let's stop any chance of this happening and establish your way of being reliably organised. This will put an end to forgetting appointments, missing sports training, handing in homework late, accidentally standing up your friends, or forgetting or missing important deadlines.

I write in a big black diary. You might prefer to use your phone, tablet, laptop, etc. Anything is fine, as long as you have a reliable system that works for you and makes it easy to record all your commitments, appointments and important things to do. Although it might seem a nuisance at the time, get things recorded in your diary or set a reminder straight away. It's no-one else's responsibility and it's great to feel organised.

> *I was talking with a friend recently who shared a story involving his teenage son, who was unsure of his direction after high school. He had discussed many options with his parents, the careers advisors at school and his friends. After a great deal of research and loads of time spent*

agonising over the options, the son finally decided to apply for a nursing degree that was offered at the local university.

There was a conversation between father and son about what was required to enrol, including filling in the application for the entrance exam. When his father offered to help with that, his son said he was late to meet a friend and would do it himself later. 'There's no hurry to register,' the son thought, as the exam was a couple of months away.

On the long-awaited day for the one and only entrance exam, the father drove his son to the venue and, in passing, asked if he'd received any registration paperwork for the exam. All was quiet in the back seat, then after a moment, the son asked, 'Didn't we fill out an online form?'

He was very quickly reminded by his father about what had happened when he tried to help with that.

A chill went down the teen's spine. Yes, he had forgotten.

It was a simple mistake that had major consequences. Instead of being able to study in his home town, the son had to apply elsewhere and settle for doing a nursing degree at a university 80km away. This meant he either had to move out of home or spend two hours on the train every day.

> **Don't let something like this happen to you. Set up a reliable system that works for you so you're able to remember things.**

Plan before you move out of home

READ THIS IF YOU DON'T KNOW HOW TO WORK THE WASHING MACHINE.

Is your instinct telling you to get away from all the rules and restrictions of home and grab the first opportunity to move into a place of your own?

Maybe you've started your first year at university and love the new freedom and the fact that you're being treated as an adult. However, this all ends as soon as you arrive home; your parents seem to have missed your last six birthdays and still think you're thirteen. You qualify for living-away-from-home allowance and feel that moving into a share house would see your independence complete.

Or perhaps you have deferred from university, have a couple of jobs and have plenty of extra cash. The people you work with have become your new friendship group and a couple of them ask you to move into a unit with them and let the party begin!

All these are great reasons to move out of home, right? Maybe they are, but moving out before you're ready can also be a BIG mistake.

The following scenario is all too common. You move out with no idea how to cook or wash clothes and don't realise how much everything costs. After a couple of months, your housemates' mess, previously unnoticed mood swings and lack of help with household jobs becomes irritating. In addition, the bills keep coming, resulting in insufficient funds to finance your mission to 'go out and have fun'. Talking about the issues does nothing, and it all ends badly with housemates going their separate ways, all with empty pockets. Although this may sound negative, I have seen it happen a lot with staff at Subway.

There is an argument that struggling with bills, cooking and household chores is all life experience and learning. That no matter who you move in with, there could be difficult aspects of their personality that only come to light when you're under the one roof. And this is all true to some extent, but why not minimise these problems by doing a bit of preparation before taking the leap?

There's no rule for identifying the right time to move out, but if you feel that you're getting close to wanting to find a place of your own, pause and consider what it might really be like. While you still have all the comfort and support of a home plan, pretend you have already moved out and are on your own. Learn some basic skills: how to cook, wash clothes, go shopping on a budget, clean your house and organise bills. Also look objectively at the people you hope to move out with. Ignore the fact they're friends and focus on how they like to live, their individual habits and their everyday personalities.

If, after all that research, you still think you can live out of home and with these people, go for it: now is the time to move out, work on your independence, and take responsibility. I bet you're more likely to make a success of it. And if it still goes badly, despite all that research, you could always ask your parents if you can come home ... if they'll have you back!

> **Don't rush the decision to move out: think about it carefully and learn some domestic skills first.**

17

Find mentors and advisors

READ THIS IF YOU THINK YOU CAN DO IT ALL ON YOUR OWN. OR IF YOU KNOW YOU NEED SOME HELP.

When you're a teenager, you think you know everything. And you probably do. But that doesn't mean you won't need advice from time to time. Not being prepared to ask for advice may see you miss opportunities or struggle unnecessarily.

A mentor is somebody who can provide that guidance and advice. All sorts of people can be mentors. A favourite relative may be a mentor for a lifetime; others may come and go as your interests and situation change. Then there's the single-issue advisor whose advice you seek only for a specific matter.

> *Time for a bit of a confession here. I am pretty hopeless at computers but I'm surrounded by them. Fortunately for me I have Nardo, an old friend from school who studied computers and has been a saviour and my go-to computer man for my whole business career. Over the past thirty years I have also shared my journey with another retailer who, like myself, ran many retail stores. Unlike me, aka Mr Impatient who tends to rush into things, this friend is methodical and unaffected by my enthusiasm. He has been there for the birth of most of my business ideas and on several occasions has saved me from what would have been the wrong decision.*

Teachers can often be mentors. Perhaps school is getting you down. Maybe you're having trouble with difficult subjects, your peers or teachers. Or even all three. But let's say the relationship you have with one of your teachers is really positive. You feel understood and it's almost like they're a friend. They may be a potential mentor for your issues at school. It's possible they can help defuse any issues you have with other teachers, and you may also be surprised how much they know about the other children and the 'politics' of the schoolyard.

The most important mentors in my life are my parents. Even if they don't completely understand the complexities of a situation I still ask their opinion, because I know they will be honest and confidential, and always have my best intentions in mind. I hope your parents are mentors for you too, but as you leave home, begin tertiary study or enter the workforce, people outside your family may be the right ones to provide encouragement, useful guidance or a different perspective.

Think about areas of your life where you have challenges or important decisions to make. Is there anyone already in your life that may help? Once you start to ask for advice and help, I'm confident you will see the benefits.

Here's an example of someone young who found a mentor.

Alec came from a no-frills, hard-working and supportive family and sought his parents' advice on many matters. At a very young age, he started his own business, which grew and became increasingly successful. Alec had paid advisors, an accountant and lawyers, but there were social situations and areas of business etiquette that he struggled with. He actively sought out advice from family, friends and those around him to fill the gaps in his knowledge.

Alec found that, when asked, most people are only too pleased to help, and often flattered that you respect their knowledge. Even though his business is now well established, he still meets monthly for a coffee with a range of people who continue to support his journey.

> **Look at your life: for any area you have difficulties in, seek out people whose advice you can ask for or who may be able to help.**

18

Ask that question

READ THIS IF YOU THINK YOU'RE SUPPOSED TO KNOW IT ALL ALREADY, OR IF YOU'RE SHY AND DON'T LIKE BEING THE CENTRE OF ATTENTION.

How many times have you heard a teacher ask, 'Does everyone understand?' and, 'Are there any questions?' only to get complete silence. Then, straight after class, someone asks if you understood. It turns out they didn't understand, and neither did you. Why does this happen? Are people frightened of drawing attention to themselves or looking stupid? Not asking questions can be a huge missed opportunity.

At school, I was often the one who asked a question and I still do today. It's by far the quickest and most efficient way to learn things. Although you can read about stuff in books, listen to a podcast or do research online, it's often better to ask a real live human being a question – one who can give you the answer directly. If you're shy, or don't like drawing attention to yourself, ask the question after class or in private, and keep asking more questions until you understand fully.

Make asking questions a priority and get into the habit of doing it in all sorts of different situations. If you see someone doing something that interests you, ask if they would mind explaining it. Talk to people who have unusual jobs or a different life from yours: be genuinely interested and politely ask questions. In my experience, most people love talking about themselves or their hobby, and who knows what you might learn?

> *My need to ask questions gave me a business opportunity that changed my life. I was working in my health-food store and, although I really enjoyed my work, I knew I would never make a fortune from it. My wife was working full time, but with three young boys to care for she decided to work part time and so began the search for a way to replace the lost income. My plan was to keep the health-food store and find another business to run simultaneously. I only had a small budget and there were not many businesses in my price range, so the business agent grew used to my persistent questions.*
>
> *One morning I was in his waiting room and overheard him say to someone else that these clients were keen to sell at a bargain price. Those words were music to my ears. When it was time for my appointment, the first question I asked him was why hadn't he told me about this business? He said that one potential buyer had spent quite a while looking at the business and had eventually agreed to buy it. However, the buyer kept coming back with small issues he wanted resolved before signing the contract. So in my eyes, it was still for sale, and, persistent as ever, I asked*

what the business was and whether I could have a look at the figures. The next day and night was spent doing my research, speaking to my accountant and visiting the store many times to politely ask the staff the questions that kept popping into my head.

A day later, I had decided that this business was just what we were looking for. I asked the agent what the agreed price was and whether I could speak directly to the owners – whom I ended up talking to four times in the next two hours! They were frustrated with the hassles they'd been having with the other potential buyer, so they agreed that if I signed the contact and paid a deposit that day, the business was mine.

And so my journey in Subway stores began.

None of this would ever have occurred had I not been so persistent in asking questions.

Ask that question!

19

Be politely determined

READ THIS IS YOU'VE EVER GIVEN UP TRYING TO GET WHAT YOU WANT.

From a very early age, I got used to hearing things like:

- 'You're not allowed in.'
- 'Don't touch that.'
- 'Just wait there.'

Then, as I got older, it changed to things like:

- 'It's not my responsibility.'
- 'That's not how we do it.'
- 'Sorry, it's out of stock'.

These responses can be annoying, frustrating and sometimes unfair, so why not ask the bearer of bad news to explain further?

You may have been taught that it's not right to 'question authority', and so this may seem like a difficult thing to do. But if you have a concern about something, I think you should have your say – politely. Remember that it's easy for someone to say 'no'. In my experience, saying no means someone could be looking for the quickest way out. They might be unsure, too busy, or about to take a break. Unless you take the time to question them, and really confirm that the answer they gave you is final, you may miss the chance to get the outcome you want. If you're concerned about questioning someone older, in a uniform, or important-looking, don't be. You have nothing to lose if you've already been told no.

So let's now have a look at exactly how to do this, step by step.

- Listen carefully to the person's response to your question.
- If the answer you've been given seems wrong, unfair or unclear, ask them – politely – to clarify.
- Say that you saw it differently and ask if they can give their reasons for saying no to your original request.
- If they still say no and you remain unsatisfied, ask whether there are alternatives or if there is someone else you can speak to.

Ask everything in a respectful, non-threatening tone of voice. Be prepared to say that you're sorry for being a nuisance, that you can see they're busy, and that you really appreciate their help and effort. I've often seen a complete change in attitude with this approach, with the person taking extra time to really try to help or find a compromise.

Even if the answer really is no, or the situation cannot be changed, at least you can be satisfied you have explored all options and maybe learnt something.

Here's one of my efforts:

As a twelve-year-old my dream was to own a mini bike and I spent hours researching them in books and magazines. Just a couple of small problems – I had no money and my parents were completely against the idea.

Not to be deterred, I hatched a plan. Dad was a self-employed tradesman, and as the school holidays were approaching I asked if I could earn some pocket money by working with him on some of his jobs. This worked a treat, as Dad secretly hoped that one day I might become his apprentice and Mum was keen for me to develop a work ethic. So for those holidays, and at every opportunity, I was Dad's young apprentice and my savings grew steadily. I also left magazines about mini bikes lying around in strategic places as a politely determined way of showing that my dream was still alive.

Then – an amazing opportunity presented itself.

While working on a job with Dad I noticed in the corner of the owner's shed a dusty old mini bike. It was nothing like the ones I'd been researching, but it had two wheels and a little engine – everything I needed to make my dream come true. It instantly became the most important thing in my life, but how could I possibly make it mine? Some clever tactics were needed.

The owner of the shed where I found the bike just happened to be a friend of my father's and someone I'd met prior to this job. So rather than mention my discovery to my father, I decided to approach the owner directly. At first he was a little dismissive, saying the bike hadn't been ridden for years and he wasn't sure if it still worked. Again, I was undeterred, and with a mix of fear and excitement I asked if he would be interested in selling it. To my great joy he said yes. It was just sitting in the shed, so why not? Now on a roll I asked how much he wanted for it. He asked how much I had saved. I told him, and his next words were music to my ears: 'Well, that's the price then.'

Some initial success. Now it was time to ask my parents.

The next day, before Dad came home from work, I told

Mum the whole story. As I expected, the response wasn't positive. But I couldn't give up now. I explained that it was only a very little mini bike, that I had enough money to pay for it myself, and as it needed a little bit of love it would be a great project to do with my granddad. To my great surprise she agreed that I could have the bike, but I knew Dad would be a tougher assignment.

As expected, he started firing questions at me and putting obstacles in my way. 'The owner might still use it,' 'It might not go,' 'It might not be for sale,' 'How would you pay for it?' Little did Dad know, I had anticipated all these questions and had solid answers. But then he rolled out the big guns and said there was no way known that Mum would agree to let me have the bike. But I had my answer ready and told him she had already given permission. I knew I was over the line, and the next day the mini bike was in our garage.

> **My polite determination paid off ...
> now have a go yourself.**

Can they help me succeed?

READ THIS IF YOU WANT TO GET AHEAD.

You may have heard the saying, 'I wish I had known that when I was your age.' Because I'm well past being 'a young one', I know what a great source of help, support and guidance the people you meet every day can be. Family, friends, sporting coaches, school teachers, and even people you have just met can help you in all sorts of surprising ways if you take the trouble to ask.

Every time you meet someone, think, 'Is there a question I'd like to ask them, something I could learn from them, or is there some support they could give me?' At first you may be shy and not want to be a bother, but in my experience, people are willing to help and even flattered that you have asked for their assistance, opinion or advice.

These conversations can really help with the challenge of deciding what you would like to do when you leave school. Every person you meet is a case study. Try asking things like:

- 'How did you get into that?'
- 'Do you enjoy it?'
- 'What are the job prospects like?'

If you're already studying they might be able to help you with career direction, work experience or connections.

Here's a classic example of somebody making the most of the people they meet:

> I know a young AFL player who is a great example of someone who creates relationships with the people he meets. Most of his time is spent training, recovering, in meetings, preparing for matches, or playing on match day. But there's a whole other side to being an AFL footballer: school and community camps, Auskick, hospital visits, sponsor dinners, community appearances and functions are all a big part of their lives. Many players would rather hang out and do their own thing, and see these commitments as annoying because they must be on their best behaviour and represent the club. But unlike some of his fellow footballers, the player I know sees these 'annoyances' as opportunities. He recognises that people around football clubs are very keen to help players and share their experience: often beyond what you would normally expect. During a post-match function, he met a sponsor who works in an area of interest for him. He took the time to have a discussion and showed a genuine curiosity. The following week they met for a coffee, and the sponsor arranged for the player to visit their offices.

Because he had shown so much genuine enthusiasm, he was offered a couple of days of work experience with the sales team and, again, the player took the opportunity to ask questions and learn. After several more visits and discussions with management, the player was offered a custom-made position that allowed him to go in once a week for training and experience. It was a real head start for a job after football.

This contact and opportunity could have gone in an instant had this player not taken the time and interest. Do the same yourself every chance you get.

> **Take an interest in those around you and how they might be able to support you. You have nothing to lose.**

21

Go straight there – not sideways

READ THIS IF YOU PREFER TO SNEAK UP ON THINGS

We all have problems or issues in our lives that need our attention in order to get them sorted. Perhaps you feel you're being unfairly left out of a team or maybe you've bought faulty jeans and the sales people won't let you return them.

You may have heard people say, 'You will need to go about things in the right way.' That there is a step-by-step process that cannot be changed. This may be true in certain cases, but if something is important to me I rarely accept this. I was recently told there was no chance of getting my passport renewed to meet a deadline, but I managed to sort it out.

When you have an issue or problem to solve, always ask yourself, 'What is the most efficient way to sort this out?' If someone tells you to handle a problem or situation in a certain way, I would encourage you to not just accept this at face value. You may eventually have to fall into line and follow a set procedure, but test it first – politely, of course. Generally, going directly to the most senior person available will make your journey to a satisfactory solution shorter. But doing this can be awkward, so you might want to go halfway first by speaking to someone junior and making a tentative, inoffensive enquiry. At least you can say you had a go. Unfortunately, the common response to this sort of enquiry is, 'Leave it with me and I'll see what I can do.' But usually this is just code for, 'Don't hold your breath – nothing will get done.' Don't be deterred, keep looking for the next senior person to ask and you will be amazed at how often you will succeed.

For example, have you been trying to get a part-time job for a while? Have you been following the same pattern of handing your resume to the first employee you see and asking them to 'pass it on'? The chances are it went straight in the bin. Instead, go as far into the store as possible without getting into trouble for trespassing, and ask to have a quick word with the most senior person there. If you get the feeling that the manager's not around, return later and try again. It's worth the effort because a short meeting with a manager gives you a chance to leave a positive impression. Another approach, which always impresses me, is to hand in your resume anyway, but return a couple of days later to confirm with the manager that he or she received it.

Another example is if you've been overlooked for sport, debating, or the end-of-year production. Try the same approach: go directly to the coach, teacher or organiser, speak to them respectfully, and explain that you feel you'd have heaps to offer had you been selected. You have nothing to lose, and everything to gain. While you're there ask if there is any chance of them changing their mind. Who knows – because of your enthusiasm they may reconsider including you or create another spot for you. If nothing else, they're certain to take more notice of you next time.

> It doesn't matter what the situation is, if you think you've been given a raw deal or treated unfairly, don't just accept it – take it further. Seek out the most senior person with the power to change the situation and put across your case in a determined, but polite and respectful way.

ADVANCED

So this is where the smallest of actions can have the biggest of impacts. You may have nodded your head at some of the suggestions made in earlier chapters, thinking you already knew that or already do that. That may also be the case for what follows and if so, well done, but I suspect for many it may not be. Whatever the case, read carefully and have a go at taking the following suggestions on board. All of them will help your progress at school, at university, at work and, most importantly, in life in general.

Keep your moods to yourself

READ THIS IF YOU'RE GRUMPY AND CAN'T BE BOTHERED.

Controlling your moods now is important, but it becomes even more important when you leave school and enter the workforce.

You may have seen babies throwing tantrums and screaming with their arms and legs going everywhere, only to be smiling and playful a short while later. Babies' emotions are raw and untouched and no amount of adult reasoning seems to stop them. It's natural for babies – it's their way of communicating without words. They're very good at attracting the attention of the people around them and using their screams to get what they want. This might make parents angry, upset, frustrated or embarrassed, but all is forgiven with the next smile. Babies, quite rightly, can get away with moodiness. But from then on there may be a price to pay.

As we get older, what is expected of us changes. Unfortunately, some people continue to let everyone around them know how they feel. Unlike babies, this moodiness is not forgiven quite so readily when you're older, and affects not just that moment but how people see you in the longer term. There is no point being all smiles today then miserable tomorrow: one doesn't cancel the other out.

At school, there may be few consequences for being moody, grumpy and ignoring people – it's no big deal and no-one else's business, right? Maybe, maybe not. Even at school being moody can have its impact. Friends may avoid you, you might get in trouble with teachers, or you might miss out on being chosen for a team or excursion.

If you have a job, controlling your moods starts to become really important. Customers are not interested in your moods or what's causing them. They just want the same friendly service every time. Isn't that reasonable?

You might disagree. You might argue that it's not your fault: you're unable to control your emotions and you've tried changing, but it's just your personality and you have difficult things going on in your life. But guess what – most people have problems, but you would never know because they leave those problems at home.

I know of many situations in life and the workplace where people have been overlooked for an opportunity or have been labelled as grumpy because they cannot control their moods.

> *Some years ago I had a girl working for us at Subway who had many of the skills needed to be a manager.*

She was efficient, neat, punctual and well organised. Unfortunately she would have all too regular 'grumpy days' and I could tell as soon as I saw or spoke to her that it was one of those days. We tried all sorts of strategies to encourage her to manage these days, as it affected how she treated customers, other staff and sometimes even me. Unfortunately we did not have any great success and on this single issue she missed an opportunity to manage a store.

At Subway, we have some methods for helping people who struggle with leaving their bad moods at home. We ask them to create an 'at-work mood' by combining their happiest and grumpiest mood, finding the middle, and using that. It might sound simplistic, but it works for us. Another approach to a 'struggle day' is to try being 100% smiley and upbeat for the first ten seconds. This will create the mood for you, and then you can relax and just be pleasant.

The most memorable impression people have of you can be your bad moods. Once you're labelled it can be hard to change. Have a go at these suggestions, and think, 'How would this person like me to speak to them?', 'Would

I like being around myself right now?', and 'Nobody likes a grump.'

> **Managing your moods is worth the effort as your behaviour not only affects how you get along with people, but can also determine how you are perceived and even what opportunities you are given.**

Listen before you speak

READ THIS IF YOU TALK TOO MUCH, OR IF YOU THINK YOU CAN READ MINDS.

When my wife reads this she'll laugh, as it's a classic case of someone not 'practising what they preach'. I admit, I can sometimes be impatient in a conversation and start answering questions before the other person has finished talking because I've guessed what's coming next. This can be rude and annoying for the other person, and it's especially awkward when your guess about what the other person was trying to say is wrong!

There are a few reasons why people interrupt. You may know the other person well and feel certain you know what's coming next, so there's no need to hear it. Or maybe it's something you don't want to hear. Some people interrupt to try to impress you with their knowledge of the topic, while others may think you're taking too long to say what you have to say and are too impatient to wait any longer. None of these are a valid reason to interrupt. You should always wait until the sentence or point being made is finished. Not only is it rude to interrupt, but you may miss out on something that's important or beneficial to you.

On the other hand, this doesn't mean you can't be involved and acknowledge what's being said. Have an expression that matches the mood of conversation or acknowledge the points with a gentle nod. A few 'mmm's' and 'ah ha's' and the occasional, 'Yes, I see,' also show that you're interested without interrupting the other person's train of thought.

> I clearly recall the first time I was invited to a teenage party. I was dead keen to go but knew getting this past my parents was going to be a very difficult task. I was predicting questions about alcohol, whether there would be adult supervision, etc. So I thought my best approach would be to think of every negative question my parents had and prepare a good answer. The best defence is a good offence.
>
> The early part of the conversation went as planned. My parents started with the where, what time, who's going, etc., and then went on to the negative details. As I thought I knew where the conversation was going, I leapt in, all guns blazing, with all my defensive answers, even to questions that hadn't been asked! Unlike me, my parents waited until I had finished what I had to say, and guess what they said – 'If you had given us the chance to finish with our concerns, we were going to say yes anyway.'

This was a very good lesson for me.

> Practise not interrupting until the end of the sentence. Instead, listen carefully and then make your reply. It's a great skill to have.

Treat everybody as important

READ THIS IF YOU'RE RICH OR POOR OR ANYTHING IN BETWEEN.

I grew up in a household where anyone who wore a suit and tie was seen as important. Most of the people around us wore overalls and we rarely had dealings with people in a suit, so when we did, my parents would dress and present themselves at their best.

When I was a young boy, the wearing of a suit and tie became a benchmark for how important somebody was. Of course, I can now see how misguided my childhood view was, and have since learnt that to measure the importance of people by such things as how they dress, how they speak or where they went to school is a big mistake.

I think it's much better to try to recognise the individual skills and achievements of all equally: if you're sick, the most important person might be the doctor; if your car has broken down on a dark, rainy night, it's easy to elevate the status of the soon-to-arrive roadside repairer to 'demi-god'.

Many of us also spend time trying to impress and associate with people in authority, or people we see as successful, hoping that we might benefit somehow or that some of their success might 'rub off' on us.

But I think it's a better idea to treat everyone you come across with respect and genuine interest. With this approach, you will get the best from everyone you meet and potentially give great pleasure to people who aren't used to being given respect. You may also find that, without even trying, doors open and opportunities come your way.

> *My first business was a very small specialist hardware store. I had little money and therefore was neither a volume buyer nor was I able to carry much stock. During a visit to my main supplier, I was introduced to the owner. He seemed very important, and as I was a tiny customer I received little attention. I suppose that, in his eyes, I wasn't worth the effort.*
>
> *So instead of trying to impress the big boss, I wandered over to where the products were dispatched and had a conversation with the storemen about their boss's rather indifferent welcome. I joked that the storemen and line workers were the real bosses of the business, as nothing left or arrived without them knowing about it. They responded by taking an interest in me, asking about my business and offering a few simple, but important, suggestions.*
>
> *As time went by, I spoke to the storemen more often. When I placed orders or checked delivery dates with them, I always treated them with the same sense of fun*

and respect. One year, just before Christmas, I quoted on a large order and was disappointed when the tender went to a competitor. But then the purchaser rang to say that my competitor was unable to supply before Christmas, and that if I could somehow pull off the impossible and fill the order before Christmas it was mine.

I knew the warehouse had closed their orders for the holidays and there was little hope, but it was my biggest order of the year and I was desperate to get it. I rang my favourite person in orders to be told what I already knew – that I was too late. I jokingly pleaded with him to see if there was any chance he could sneak my order through. To my great joy, all the genuine goodwill, interest and, most importantly, respect that I had shown towards them paid off, and they dispatched the order that afternoon.

I had a very happy customer who went on to purchase many more items for their home.

Have a go at treating everybody as important; it's easy!

Cuddle angry people into happiness

READ THIS IF YOU LIKE TO FIGHT FIRE WITH FIRE.

Whether you have to do it face to face or on the phone, dealing with someone who has steam coming out of their ears can be a challenge. People can become grumpy at almost anything: poor customer service, faulty products, or the fact that you did this or said that. Often they don't even give you a chance to offer your point-of-view on the situation. Sound familiar?

Some people's standard response to anger is to fight fire with fire, but this is likely to result in a major argument. Instead, although it may seem unnatural, why not do the opposite: be nice to the person who is angry and encourage them to have their say. You will be amazed at how a 'verbal cuddle' has the potential to soothe their anger.

When people are angry they're convinced that they're right, so your aim is to settle the conversation down so you can explain your perspective, seek a compromise or, if necessary, apologise in a way that is genuine.

You might have tried to do this in the past, but found you're unable to carry it through – you might stay calm for a while but end up blowing up anyway. Then it still ends with a shouting match, and you probably feel worse as you're now also angry with yourself for giving in. So instead of trying to grin and bear these situations, let's look at a detailed plan for handling them.

- Keep a comfortable distance from the person, or telephone, but be close enough to be heard when speaking in a polite, gentle tone. Allow the angry person to explain their whole issue without interrupting them, but confirm any key points by gently nodding your head at important moments or saying things like, 'So, your food was cold?'

- If at any stage they ask you to agree with what they're saying, use phrases like, 'I'm sorry you feel that way,' or, 'Would you mind if I check and get back to you?' If, from your perspective, they're being ridiculous, it's okay to calmly say, 'I'm sorry, but that's not the way I saw it,' and look for any point of compromise.

- Be mindful of your tone of voice and body language. This is vital. Maintain an even tone of voice, take an interest in what's being said and, where appropriate, say things like, 'I hear what you're saying.' Should the situation lighten a little, change your tone to match and relax the situation. If you're unsure of anything regarding their issue, it's better to admit this.

- If you sense that their anger is too intense to settle quickly, carefully suggest that you discuss the matter later. Continue to acknowledge their anger and that what they have to say is being taken seriously.

Letting the person get their concerns off their chest while you remain calm often results in the person settling down, being open to compromise or even changing their mind. They may have only wanted to have their say and be heard, or wanted something explained to them properly. If you're in the wrong and you can make a genuine apology, it's likely to be well received and everybody can move forward.

Unfortunately, this approach is not always successful, as some people are simply looking for someone to take their anger out on. The anger they feel often has nothing to do with the immediate situation, which helps explain why they're angry at something that seems trivial. In this situation remember that it's not about you – you just happened to be in the firing line when the person needed to vent.

> **By taking this approach you will avoid many confrontations and ultimately even gain respect for your rational approach.**

Treat others like yourself

READ THIS IF YOU THINK IT'S ALL ABOUT YOU.

This might not seem important to you now, but very soon you will be entering a world where the way you treat others is important. It affects how you're seen by others and influences the opportunities you're offered.

Most of the staff in our restaurants are still at school and working at Subway is often their first job. One major thing that has to be learnt quickly is that practical jokes, which are seen as 'harmless fun' at school, are not tolerated in the workplace. Unacceptable behaviour such as bullying, victimisation and racism do happen at school, but once in the workforce there can be real consequences, resulting in civil or even criminal charges.

As part of all new-staff training, we point out that treating people unfairly, talking about others behind their back, leaving them out, or just being rude has no place at work or in society in general. We promise new staff that we will always treat them with 'the greatest respect' and in turn they must do the same for other staff and customers. We acknowledge that everyone has their strengths and weaknesses, so we praise the things they're good at and help them improve anything they're not so good at.

Whether or not these suggestions are already how you see things, here is the challenge.

Next time you come into contact with someone you see as a little out of the ordinary, put yourself in their shoes. Think how you would like to be treated and spoken to if you were them. Then, have a go at doing just that and watch their response: you will see their appreciation, and maybe even surprise, that someone took the time to care. Your thought and effort can bring real pleasure to others.

Speaking to people like this may have all sorts of unintended consequences.

> At school, I had plenty of material for kids to tease me about: red hair, big black glasses and being a bit overweight. My response was to ignore the kids who tried to tease me and keep out of their way, and so for me it was no big deal. But for others who were being bullied it was, so I made the effort to speak to and support these people.
>
> One of the boys in my year at high school had a very 'out-there' fashion sense and was often teased and left to himself. I found him fascinating and very funny as he had his own views on the kids who teased him. He was an

excellent judge of people, and I enjoyed listening to his ideas and plans for the future.

A few years ago I unexpectedly met him again in an airport lounge and, although thirty years had passed since we had been at school, we both recognised each other. We were on the same delayed flight, and were able to spend some time having a good chat and reflecting on our days at high school – the good and the bad. He revealed that although he never said so at school, he really appreciated that I accepted him for who he was, spent time with him, and offered support regardless of what anyone else said. I had never given this any thought, but he clearly had, and over a long period of time. After school he left all those bad experiences behind and went into the adult world with a new set of rules. He became a flight attendant, completed a degree and is now the head of human resources for a major airline.

Our unexpected meeting was a wonderful thing. He was happy to have had the chance after many years to say thanks for my support at school, and for me, it reinforced the importance of treating people as you would like to be treated yourself.

Although we live in different countries, we still keep in contact. During one conversation I mentioned that my wife and I were flying to the UK soon. When we arrived at the airport we discovered, to our great surprise and joy, that our tickets had been upgraded by my old school friend from economy to business class!

> **Take the time to experiment with 'treating others like yourself'. I'm confident it will be a great experience for both you and everybody you interact with.**

27

Always praise people

READ THIS IF YOU'RE WORRIED ABOUT SUCKING UP.

Giving praise may not be something that comes naturally to you. Maybe you're not sure what to say or how to say it. Perhaps you don't know if it's appropriate to praise somebody. However, it's almost impossible to give praise too often or in the wrong way. Praise given with sincerity has the most wonderful and positive effect on the receiver and leaves you with a great feeling of having made someone feel special.

Many of you will have already experienced the joys of giving praise. Saying 'well done' in sport, particularly team sport, seems to happen naturally. As part of a team you're working together to succeed, improve or achieve a goal. Everyone needs to be encouraged to do their best. Those who struggle the most need the most support and, from what I have seen, when they receive praise they respond with enthusiasm and often improved performance.

If you see yourself as one of the best in a team or if you excel in a group that's working together, have a go at offering genuine praise and support to those who are struggling. They might be amazed that you have bothered to encourage them and I can almost guarantee that you will see some improvement. It will be as satisfying for you as it is for them.

As I said, praising a member of a team comes fairly naturally, but let's also work on the individual.

People like your parents and school teachers are forever doing things for you. I hope I'm wrong but I suspect you rarely thank them and, even worse, they don't expect you to. Next time they help you, stop, look them in the eye, thank them for what they've done and say that you really appreciate their help. It's likely to be the best smile you will see all day and will probably encourage them to help you more often in the future.

How to receive praise

Giving praise is important, and so is receiving it well. Some people struggle with accepting praise and are not sure how they should respond; they might feel a little awkward at the attention or even dismiss it as unwarranted and offer a half-hearted, grunting reply. As hard as it may be, it's very important to be able to accept praise well, if only to acknowledge that a person has taken the time to give it to you.

The simple plan is, when someone gives you praise, reply and say thank you with the same enthusiasm as the praise was given. Then, as we do in our home, have five minutes of joy to celebrate your achievement or the fact that you've been noticed. Plenty of not-so-good stuff happens during a day, so make a point of enjoying the good stuff before you move on.

> It doesn't matter if it's someone at school or work, a family member, a friend, or someone you have just met for the first time: look for reasons to give praise. People are uplifted, perform better and feel valued.

Say thank you often

JUST READ THIS; IT'S PRETTY SHORT.

'Thank you' is a simple and powerful statement that is easy to say, but too often not said. For some people, saying thank you is just not a priority, while others forget to say it or simply can't be bothered. I have even heard people say, 'If I thank them for that I will have to thank them for everything.' Like that's a problem...

It's almost impossible to thank people too much and when delivered correctly, gratitude gives great pleasure to the receiver. For the giver, it brings the satisfaction of making someone happy. Some people can become disheartened without gratitude, and for them a sincere thank you is worth more than money.

There is no more striking example of this than in my Subway stores. Taking the time to acknowledge a really clean store or well topped-up counter, or giving a big thank you for helping cover a shift makes the person who receives it happy. But it also makes it much more likely that they will be just as helpful, hard-working and responsible in the future.

Saying thank you and expressing gratitude can do more than just create warm fuzzy feelings for everybody. It can be life changing.

I know of a young professional sportsman who has used the power of gratitude to create and cement a really strong relationship. He loves Nike gear, and as a junior went out of his way to wear the brand. He asked for Nike gear for birthday and Christmas presents, and also had a cousin who played sport professionally and was able to supply some 'hand-me-down' gear. This saw him rarely without a Nike logo.

During a function at his club, the young sportsman met a Nike executive and, as usual, he was wearing Nike gear. During their exchange, he shared his loyalty to the brand and asked questions about the company's products. At the end of their conversation, the player thanked the executive for enduring his interrogation. He was later asked if he would like to call by their head office, have a tour and look at the latest range. Of course, he said yes.

This visit was a great success, with the executive enjoying the young player's enthusiasm and knowledge of Nike products. His genuine appreciation had clearly been noted as, on his departure, he was given some free Nike gear. The executive had also become aware of the young man's struggle to purchase runners big enough in

Australia, so they arranged for some to be ordered from the USA! The following week, the runners arrived and he called in to collect them. To his surprise, he was told the Nike executive had generously labelled them no-cost. Unfortunately the executive was not there that day and the young sportsman couldn't thank him directly. But to show his sincere gratitude, he made the effort to return the following day and give his thanks in person. While there, the executive introduced him to the CEO and joked that the player knew more about Nike than he did. This helped to create a relationship based on appreciation and interest, which the player built up by helping the company with some small promotions. In return, he was looked after with sporting equipment.

At Christmas, he wrote personal thank you cards to all the people that he had been involved with at the company and included a small gift. The cards and gifts were received with appreciation – and surprise.

> **Thank people in every way you can. Gratitude has the most wonderful benefits for everybody.**

CONCLUSION

Well done and thank you for reading twenty-eight things I wish I knew when I was a teenager. I hope that in my observations you have found some useful new ideas that you can use.

My aim was to challenge, question and offer support in preparing you for the next phase of your life. Make your plans, do your research and observe others. Be determined to always search for the little things that may help you reach your full potential.

Keep in mind that your journey is unique, and while others will help, encourage and even seek to influence what you do, ultimately you are responsible for your own success.

Go for it and good luck.

ABOUT THE AUTHOR

Craig's career could best be described as an evolution rather than having had a well thought out plan. However, with the benefit of hindsight, it has given him a wealth of experience and insight that they don't teach you in school. He draws on this perspective in his role as a teenage mentor and adviser.

Despite strong academic results, and against the urgings of the school principal, Craig choose to leave high school at the end of Year 11 to undertake an apprenticeship.

From day one, his plans were to excel in all aspects of his trade and establish his own business as soon as possible. These high standards were rewarded as he won 'Apprentice of the Year' for the three years of his trade and in the final year won the top apprentice for all trades.

On the back of this, Craig was awarded a Victorian Overseas Foundation Scholarship that provided international study and training opportunities. With this award he travelled to the United Kingdom to study Victorian Home Restoration and with the knowledge gained he returned to Australia with an idea to launch his business career.

He opened his first retail store at the age of twenty-two and since then has gone on to establish and run over thirty retail and service businesses in sectors including Building and Construction, Hardware, Garden Supplies, Liquor, Health and, for nearly two decades, a large number of Subway Sandwich franchises.

Craig's view is that a major factor in the success of any business is to focus on people, not just products. The pursuit of complete customer satisfaction and the care taken with staff selection and retention is paramount. For that reason, he has personally interviewed the many hundreds of staff he has employed and takes a keen interest in their ongoing development.

The combination of all these people-based skills provides many practical ideas that Craig shares with his teenage audiences. His hope is that, by sharing these, he will make the journey of teenagers today a little easier.

ACKNOWLEDGEMENTS

This book would have remained locked away as memories had it not been for the insistence of my friend Chris Mackey that I write my thoughts down. Chris, along with his wife, Sue, have been my constant mentors and advisors.

The wonderful illustrations and cover design are the work of Ally Pedersen, who worked in our Subway stores for seven years and is now an accomplished and awarded graphic designer.

There were also many young advisors who kept me on track, in particular Izzy, Miles, Nick and my sons Sam, Hugh and Jeremy.

Thanks also to Grammar Factory and my editors, Carolyn and Jacqui, who have endured my persistence and urgency.

It's rare that anything in my life that requires organisation or logic is not touched by my business advisor, Christine, and this book is no exception.

And of course a huge thanks to my wonderful Subway staff and their inspirational and individual journeys.

Lastly and most importantly the most sincere of thanks to my wife, Jane, for without her years of love, support and tolerance it would have been impossible to gather these thoughts together.

ILLUSTRATION BY
ALLY PEDERSEN
@allypedersen

www.ingramcontent.com/pod-product-compliance
Lightning Source LLC
Chambersburg PA
CBHW040334300426
44113CB00021B/2750